BIG
IDEAS
FROM
LITERATURE

Published in 2024 by The School of Life
First published in the USA in 2024
930 High Road, London, N12 9RT

Copyright © The School of Life 2024

Illustrations © Anna Doherty
Designed and typeset by Kalee Jackson
Printed in Lithuania by Balto Print

A proportion of this book has appeared online at
www.theschooloflife.com/articles

Every effort has been made to contact the copyright holders
of the material reproduced in this book. If any have been
inadvertently overlooked, the publisher will be pleased to
make restitution at the earliest opportunity.

The School of Life publishes a range of books on essential
topics in psychological and emotional life, including
relationships, parenting, friendship, careers and fulfilment.
The aim is always to help us to understand ourselves better
– and thereby to grow calmer, less confused and more
purposeful. Discover our full range of titles, including books
for children, here: www.theschooloflife.com/books

The School of Life also offers a comprehensive therapy
service, which complements, and draws upon, our published
works: www.theschooloflife.com/therapy

www.theschooloflife.com

ISBN 978-1-915087-48-5

10 9 8 7 6 5 4 3 2 1

HOW BOOKS CAN CHANGE YOUR WORLD

BIG IDEAS FROM LITERATURE

THE SCHOOL OF LIFE PRESS

THIS BOOK of
BIG IDEAS
BELONGS TO:

....

INSIDE THIS BOOK...

INTRODUCTION

WHAT ACTUALLY IS LITERATURE?

P 8

PART ONE

THE STORY OF STORIES

P 17

The Very First Book
P 19

Books You Can Carry
P 25

How to Make Lots of
Copies of a Book
P 31

How Much Did
Books Cost?
P 35

A Simple but Brilliant
Idea about Printing
P 42

The Invention of Books
Just for Children
P 47

The Industrial
Revolution and the
Unforeseen Effects of
Making Paper
P 54

What Are Schools For?
P 59

Fantasy: A New Kind
of Story
P 65

Books and Films
P 72

PART TWO

LITERATURE AND FEELINGS

P 79

Reflection

P 82

A New Perspective

P 99

Appreciation for Life

P 117

Happy Crying

P 87

Guidance

P 105

Growing Up

P 123

Encouragement

P 93

Making Hard Subjects
Entertaining

P 112

Friendship

P 127

PART THREE

WHY DO YOU LIKE YOUR FAVOURITE BOOKS?

P 135

PART FOUR

THE FUTURE OF BOOKS

P 141

CONCLUSION

MAKING FRIENDS WITH BOOKS

P 155

WHAT ACTUALLY IS LITERATURE?

'Literature' isn't a word most people use every day – in fact, you might go for ages without ever hearing it. And maybe you feel a little confused by it. But you probably already understand the basic idea: because *literature* is just a fancy way of talking about …

stories that teach you important things.

It's an interesting combination: a story *and* – in a way – a lesson. Almost all of us *like* stories. It's something to do with how our brains work: we want to know what happens next. But lessons, on the other hand, are often *far less* exciting. A lesson is something you might *need* to understand but don't particularly want to or just find it difficult to concentrate on.

So, quite early in human history people hit on a genius idea: the idea of literature. Why not use a story to teach a lesson? Why not combine something we really like with something that's helpful but maybe a bit dull?

Soon we're going to be looking at the first story that was ever written down – it's quite fascinating and contains lots of adventures. But it's got a secret. Along the way it's cleverly teaching a big lesson; a lesson about how to be a good friend – which is one of the best things you can ever learn. When you read the story, the lesson sort of slips into your mind and stays there – even though it felt like you were just reading an adventure story.

So, what other sorts of lessons might a typical story be trying to teach you? Sometimes it might be trying to teach you a very practical skill. In the 1920s an English writer called Arthur Ransome wrote an adventure story – *Swallows and Amazons* – about some children who like sailing boats. It's rather thrilling and along the way the writer tucked in lots and lots of lessons about how to manage a small boat, and how to win a race against some bitter rivals. And more recently a writer from Malawi, William Kamkwamba, wrote a book that tells you how to build your own windmill. You'll meet William and his clever windmill in Part Two.

But practical skills are not the most common type of lessons that literature wants to teach you. Most often, literature tries to teach you how to be *wise*. Being wise is a very important kind of skill – it means being good at doing something. But it's not a practical skill. It doesn't necessarily mean being clever and learning lots of facts; it's more about understanding yourself and the world around you a bit better. It means being able to understand your feelings and getting better at dealing with the millions of problems (big and small) that come from being human and having to live with other just as complicated people.

So, what is a wise idea? To get a picture of what that means let's start by looking at people (who are sometimes ourselves) who do things that aren't particularly wise at all …

Dad has forgotten
where he put his keys

A COMMON (BUT NOT SO HELPFUL) IDEA

Panic, run around, wave arms, shout at the
rest of the family.

A WISER IDEA MIGHT BE ...

Stay calm, laugh a little, think very hard
about the last place the keys were seen and
get everyone to help look for them.

Someone at school
says something
not very nice to you

A COMMON (BUT NOT SO HELPFUL) IDEA

Feel very hurt. Imagine it's true and that
everyone hates you.

A WISER IDEA MIGHT BE ...

Wonder what's wrong with this person.
What problem have they secretly got that
makes them want to be so mean? Remind
yourself that what they said is not fair and
maybe feel a little bit sorry for them instead.

You're upset and your mum doesn't understand what's upsetting you

Shout and tell her she's mean and she'll never understand. Maybe slam a door on the way to your bedroom and stay there by yourself, feeling even more miserable.

A WISER IDEA MIGHT BE …

Take a deep breath and try to explain it clearly to your mum. Maybe she still won't understand (but maybe she will) and she might be able to help you feel better anyway.

You feel a bit lonely

A COMMON (BUT NOT SO HELPFUL) IDEA

You think everybody is having fun without you and nobody likes you.

A WISER IDEA MIGHT BE …

Make a small effort to connect with someone, even if it's just a smile or a brief 'hello' and see how that feels. Maybe they feel like you and need a friend, too. Remember, you are not alone – there are lots of people who like the same things you do.

Being *wiser* is really to do with understanding life better – and giving you ideas so that you can handle lots of different situations.

But how can a story help with that? Let's look at an example: why don't we start with a story that's really aimed at very young children. The lesson isn't very difficult, but it shows how even a simple story can teach a little bit of wisdom.

In 1918, the author Beatrix Potter, living in England, wrote a very short book called *The Tale of Johnny Town-Mouse*. It's a rather sweet story of a mouse, called Timmy, from a farm in the countryside who falls asleep in a basket of vegetables that are about to be delivered to the city. In the city, he meets Johnny Town-Mouse, who is fun and smart and very polite. But the country mouse doesn't really like living in the city – there's a scary cat and the town-mice are always madly rushing about; so Timmy goes back to the quiet life in the country. Then Johnny comes from the city to the

farm for a holiday – but he gets frightened of the cows and he finds it all a bit dull; so he goes back to the city. And that's really the story.

What this story shows us is that different people (or mice!) like different things, and that's OK. Johnny likes city life and Timmy likes the countryside, and when they try out each other's lives they feel scared, uncomfortable and out of place. Maybe to you that's not a very exciting idea, you probably understand it already. But how did you learn it? Perhaps by meeting other people, going to school or even reading a similar book.

The story helps because it *shows* different little mice liking different things. It's teaching a wise idea through a sweet story.

That's for younger children – but what about a more complicated story? *The Boy at the Back of the Class*, by Onjali Raúf, is a modern story about a mysterious new boy, called Ahmet, who arrives at a school in London one day. He doesn't say anything, he doesn't look at anyone and he doesn't go into the playground at lunch or break time. He just sits at the back of the class.

But some of the other children *think* they know all about him: someone 'knows' he's been expelled from his last school and he's so dangerous he's not allowed in the playground; another is sure that Ahmet is from a very wealthy family and he's hiding at their school to escape from kidnappers. If you were in the class with Ahmet, how might you feel? What might you think about him?

It's pretty understandable that some people jump to conclusions. But they are just making assumptions – they don't really know anything about Ahmet. A really interesting option is just saying: 'I don't know what he's like yet. I can see he's shy but I don't know why. I don't know who he is, but I'd like to find out by getting to know him.'

It turns out that Ahmet is a refugee from Syria. He's been through some very horrible experiences, but eventually he makes some very good friends at school and some amazing things start happening.

It's a funny thing: it can be really helpful to say 'I don't know'.

The problem is you quite often feel you are supposed to know already. It can sound more exciting and impressive to say 'I know' than to say 'Actually I don't know'.

Often the wise ideas that literature wants to teach aren't *new*. Beatrix Potter – with her story about the mice – was probably inspired by the ancient collection of Greek stories known as Aesop's Fables. And Onjali Raúf, with the story about Ahmet at the back of the class, could also draw comparisons with an idea from an Ancient Greek philosopher called Socrates who lived more than 2,000 years ago. Socrates was famous for saying: *'The only thing I know is that I know nothing.'*

It's a funny and important thing about *wise* ideas. They might have been around for a long time but we need reminding of them. That's why we need great stories to keep on beaming wise ideas back into our brains.

So, that's what *this* book is all about. It's about finding out all the wise ideas that lots of different books (some of them very surprising) are trying to teach you via a story – and how these ideas can help you.

THE STORY OF STORIES

THE STORY OF STORIES

In terms of human history, books are a relatively recent invention. Although humans have been telling long, elaborate stories and discussing ideas for at least 70,000 years, books have only existed for around 5,000 years.

These first 'books' were clay tablets and papyrus scrolls, but even they were extremely rare. Although the invention of the printing press in the 15th century made books considerably less rare, books as we know them today – easily available in most countries – are very recent: they've only been around less than 150 years.

Publishing houses started springing up at the end of the 19th and the start of the 20th century and mass market paperbacks really took off in the 1950s. So, how did we get here? How did we go from hardly any books to billions of books – in libraries, schools, shops, warehouses, on people's shelves at home or even propping up wonky table legs?

Who invented books and what did they use them for?

Mesopotamia, Around 4,000 Years Ago

The Very First Book

One of the first things that can, at a stretch, be thought of as a book was produced in Mesopotamia (now known as Iraq). Although people had been telling each other stories for many thousands of years before this, what was special – and pretty amazing – was that they started asking a great question: what if you forget the story someone has been telling? Is there some kind of way of setting down a story so that you can go back and read it again later?

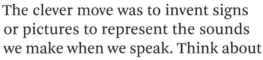 

The clever move was to invent signs or pictures to represent the sounds we make when we speak. Think about the sound 'a': in English it could be the start of the word 'animal' or it could be the sound you make in the middle of the word 'hat'. They decided to use a special mark (which looks a little bit like an arrow) to represent each sound.

 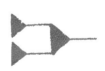

It was hard work learning all the signs, but if you did, you could read them and understand what had been written down and the sounds you should say.

They had solved *one* of the big problems that needed to be overcome in order to make books: they worked out how to write things down. But that wasn't enough. The next problem was, what do you write *on?* They didn't have any paper, because it hadn't been invented yet.

What they did was to make tablets out of wet clay and then used a little pointy implement called a stylus, made out of reeds, metal or bone, to make marks on the soft surface. Then they'd leave the clay tablets to dry in the sun until they were hard and the marks couldn't be rubbed away if you touched them.

Although it was an incredibly clever way of writing, there were several drawbacks, especially for storytellers. Clay tablets were heavy, could break easily and, unless you made an absolutely enormous one, you needed a lot of them to write a good story. The oldest piece of literature, an epic poem rediscovered in the mid-19th century, was written this way. It's not that long (you could read it in about half an hour) but it still covers twelve bulky tablets. You'd need a wheelbarrow to carry it around – not very convenient for reading in bed. It's a good story though. It's called *The Epic of Gilgamesh.*

The Epic of Gilgamesh, c.2100–1200 BCE

Making An Unexpected Friend

So, what is the story? (By the way, 'epic' means a poem or story about the adventures of a legendary hero or about events that happen over a long period of time.) Gilgamesh is a king – part-human, part-god – and although he's wise, brave and builds many things, he doesn't care much about others and does whatever he likes.

The other main character in the story is called Enkidu: he's wild and hairy and lives like an animal. Gilgamesh and Enkidu are very different and their first instinct is to fight each other. Gilgamesh proves to be stronger, but afterwards they become friends and set out on epic adventures together.

It's a wonderful and unexpected idea – you can (like Gilgamesh) be too focused on the rules. You are so worried about doing what you think is the right thing that you forget what you actually would like to do or what might be best for others. But you can (like Enkidu) be too silly: you forget that some rules might really be quite sensible. You need the other person to 'balance' you. If you only ever had friends who were just like you, you'd never get the chance to develop properly. But it's not easy: if someone's very different you might be worried they won't like you. To help, try taking the Epic of Gilgamesh unexpected-friendship test …

○ What kind of person is quite different to you?

○ How do you feel about that person? Do you dislike them? Do you (very) secretly think they might be quite interesting?

○ Can you imagine being friends with them?

○ If you did become friends with them, what would you learn from them?

○ Imagine *they* were taking the Gilgamesh test: what might they (very) secretly think about you? Maybe they are wishing they could get to be friends with you.

It doesn't mean you can't still be friends with people who are like you. Of course, that's very nice. It's just that there are other good and important kinds of friendship as well.

Isn't it amazing that the very first story ever written down – thousands of years ago – is talking about something that can still be a big issue in your life now?

Egypt, Around 3,500 Years Ago

Books You Can Carry

An Egyptian pharaoh is old and near to death. His huge burial pyramid is ready, but the pharaoh isn't worried about dying, he's worried about what happens *after* that. The Ancient Egyptians believed that important people didn't actually die at all, they went on a journey to another world located far away – maybe under the earth or in the sky – where they lived as a friend of the gods and would be happy forever.

That sounds great, but to reach the other world the pharaoh would need to get past various monsters who block the route and go through lots of gates guarded by ferocious creatures. Luckily, there's a way of dealing with them: saying certain things – a bit like very complicated passwords – that would calm the guards down and make them let him through. He would have to tell them, for example, that he didn't do anything wrong in his life or that he isn't afraid of them or that he respects them so they should respect him. But he has to know *exactly* the right words and phrases for each one: each guard and each monster needs to be told different things. If he knows the right words he'll be OK.

The Egyptian pharaohs were very worried about making this journey successfully: that's why their pyramid tombs were stuffed with things to help them, such as special food to eat, things to drink, maybe even a boat because they might need to cross a river at some point. But what about all the special words and things they needed to say?

The instructions were written in the very special way that the Ancient Egyptians had developed: they used pictures called *hieroglyphs* to represent words and ideas. It's a curious word, 'hieroglyph': it means sacred carving because the messages about how to speak to gods and spirit-guards were originally carved into stone. So at least they had instructions.

But there was a problem. You could take the special food, drink and even the boat *with* you on the journey – but what about the instructions as to what to say? They'd be back on the walls of the tomb – what if you forgot exactly what to say?

The Egyptians needed something they could write the instructions on that was also easy to carry around. Fortunately, the solution was something very close at hand – papyrus. Most Egyptian cities were built along the river Nile and papyrus reeds grew plentifully along its banks. The Egyptians discovered that the reeds could be made into a light, durable material, like thick paper, that was great for writing on. They could then paint the hieroglyphs on that and then roll it up to make a scroll. Now, they could carry the instructions around and read them whenever or wherever they needed to.

The Book of the Dead, c.1650 BCE

Words Are Powerful

These scrolls telling pharaohs what to say at the crucial moments on their journey became known as *The Book of the Dead*. Every pharaoh got their own priests to come up with new (and hopefully slightly better) instructions, so no two versions of the book (or scroll) were quite the same. It's quite a reassuring thought – imagine that a book of instructions was written not just for everyone but specifically, by experts, just for you. And over time, more and more versions were written and they stopped just being for pharaohs – it became more common to have your own book about what to do on your way to your future life.

As much as you might be curious about what the Ancient Egyptians thought, you're not actually a pharaoh and there's no reason at all to think that some day you are going to have to pass through gates guarded by spirits and monsters. So, how can what *they* wrote about on their scrolls matter in *your* life now?

The big thing the Egyptians understood is that words are powerful. You know it from your own experience: if someone says something very kind to you, it gives you a lovely warm feeling; if they say something very mean it can make you feel sad and low. If you get very angry and shout, it (usually) makes the situation worse for everyone.

In real life you have to face lots of tricky situations every day, so how helpful would it be to know exactly what to say? Suppose one of your friends is angry with you, but you didn't actually do the thing they are annoyed about. A book could help you; it might say, 'Don't get angry, stay calm; as nicely as you can, explain your point of view'. With well-chosen words you can navigate a lot of tricky situations. Or, if you *have* done something you regret and you're really sorry about it, you can make a proper apology: thoughtful words can show the other person that you really are sorry and probably (or at least hopefully) they'll forgive you.

You could make your own book – your Book of Life, maybe – listing the kind of obstacles you have to face in your journey through this world and the clever, helpful things you might say to get you past them.

○ What tricky situations do you have to face, where the right words could maybe help? For example, when you worry a grown-up is annoyed or when you feel a bit left out at school or when you are fed up with having to do your homework.

○ What instructions would you give to yourself?

○ Could you try writing them down?

○ If you don't want other people to read them you could make up your own hieroglyph pictures: three wavy lines (standing for a furrowed brow) might be a cross parent; a messy squiggle might mean 'my bedroom floor is all covered in stuff'; two hands joined together could secretly mean 'I promise' and a simple square might mean 'Everything is tidy' joined to a little arrow, which could mean 'Soon'.

As you grow you'll meet new problems and then you can think of different kinds of clever things to say so you can get through them.

China, Around 600 CE

How to Make Lots of Copies of a Book

In the earliest days of scrolls, if you wanted a book someone would need to write it out by hand for you, which would take a *very* long time. But then, in 600 CE, someone in China had a brilliant idea. Instead of copying the words by hand, they made wooden carvings of whole sections and used ink to *print* on to paper.

It was quite a tricky process. To make one of these printing blocks, they had to write on a flat block of wood and then, carefully, use a sharp blade to cut away the surrounding areas, so only the words were left. Next, they brushed ink over the wood, to cover the words. Finally, they pressed a piece of paper on top of the wood and the ink was transferred to the paper, giving them a copy of the original text.

A professional printer could print more than 2,000 sheets from one block. It was *much* faster than copying things by hand.

This is the oldest-known form of printing and although Chinese printers woodblock-printed many scrolls in the 600s, mostly about religion, sadly no copies have survived.

The Diamond Sutra, c.868 CE

A Book of Good Advice

The oldest printed book (well, scroll, actually) in the world that still exists today was produced on 11th May 868 CE for a man called Wang Jie, using the woodblock technique you've just read about. (We know the date because it's printed on the first page, which also tells us Wang Jie had the book made for his parents.) The book has a very special name: it's called *The Diamond Sutra*.

It sounds cool, but what does it mean? A sutra (meaning 'thread') is a book containing important teachings, usually from Buddhism. So, in essence it's a book about how to live your life. How great could that be? Wouldn't it be good to have some clues about what really matters? How do you know what really matters and what is just weighing us down and holding us back, without actually being important at all? Some people might be preoccupied with how they look, what they wear or what phone they have, but does that really matter?

This is where the 'Diamond' part comes in. The book's full title is actually 'The Diamond That Cuts Through Illusion'. Diamonds are really hard minerals that (apart from making fancy jewellery) are used in the toughest cutting and drilling machines in the world – a diamond blade can cut through metal and concrete! So the idea of *The Diamond Sutra* is that this book can cut through all the confusion and nonsense and tell you what you need to do to be happy and good.

So, what advice does it give? It wants to teach us all how to be happier. It wants you to care less about buying new things or passing exams or what so-and-so said. It says our ideas about what's important are sometimes a bit wrong. We think if only I could get this dress or the newest device or do really well in maths then I'll be happy. The Diamond Advice-Book wants to cut through our usual obsessions and explains that these aren't really the things that make us feel good about ourselves; the real things might be looking at the stars, being kind to someone or getting lost in our own thoughts.

This isn't really a book you have to even agree with. What's exciting is it makes you think (as all the best books do) and suggests something that you can do yourself. You could write your own version, your own special collection of advice. What would you want to explain to other people?

○   What's important? What's overrated?

○   What big mistakes do you think people might make?

○   What do you sometimes get obsessed with that doesn't really bring the happiness you imagine it will?

You don't have to decide everything now; you can change your mind or maybe it just takes a long time to work out what you really think, but you are starting on a wonderful, life-long project.

Just a little side note, *The Diamond Sutra* talks about a big and very old religion (or a philosophy; that is, a way of being wise) called Buddhism. But you don't have to call yourself a Buddhist just because you think it talks about some interesting and helpful ideas.

Europe, the Middle Ages

How Much Did Books Cost?

For a very long time, people living in different parts of the world knew little – or even nothing – about each other and how they lived. So, although woodblock printing had been used in China since the 600s, this way of making books didn't develop in Europe until hundreds of years later. Instead, in the period known as the Middle Ages (or medieval period, roughly from the end of the Roman Empire in the 5th century to around the 14th century) people in Europe continued to copy books by hand! And, instead of using paper (which the Chinese had also invented but Europeans didn't know about yet) they wrote on very thin pieces of animal skin, called parchment or vellum.

However, rather than joining together the pieces of leather in a long strip and rolling them into a scroll, they had the idea of sewing the pieces together along one side. This meant, for the first time, you could turn the pages instead of unrolling a scroll.

It might not seem such a big deal – what's so hard about using a scroll? A scroll is fine if it's short, but if it's long it could be quite tricky. Suppose you want to go back to check something at the beginning or sneak ahead and see what happens at the end: you'd have to spend ages rolling and unrolling the scroll with both hands and you'd probably end up crumpling it. With pages it's so much easier.

Another important thing about books from the Middle Ages, and many do survive today, is that most of them were very beautiful. Many pages were highly decorated and beautifully illustrated – making the book a piece of art to be looked at as well as something to read. They used rich, strong colours, with paint made from colourful minerals and plants, and the most luxurious books were 'illuminated' with silver and gold paint or even gold leaf. If you were reading at night (by candlelight, of course), it must have been like looking into a magical, shimmering world.

The big idea was that *beauty* is very appealing. You want to keep on paying attention to things you find very, very nice to look at. So, by making a book beautiful, people would be more likely to want to read it – and learn the lesson that the book was hoping to teach.

As you can imagine, these amazing books would have been very expensive. But, back then, very few people could read anyway because education was only for the rich. Most books were made by monks (it would have taken them ages!) and kept in monastic libraries, where the books were often chained to the shelves to stop people stealing them.

The Westminster Abbey Bestiary, 1275-1290 CE

What We Can Learn from Animals

Let's look a bit more closely at one of the most beautiful, handwritten books from the Middle Ages. This one is called a 'bestiary' – which, is not as you might think, a book about things that are the 'best'. It means a book about 'beasts'; but before you start imagining all kinds of scary or dangerous creatures, in the Middle Ages 'beast' simply meant 'animal'. (It could mean real animals or mythical ones though; people weren't too sure which animals really existed!)

Nowadays we know lots about animals from all over the world, but it was different in the Middle Ages. Most people didn't travel too far from the town they'd been born in. So, while they knew a lot about some animals, like pigs, sheep and horses (as they were important sources of food or transport), they were probably not too interested in reading about them (if they could read). But stories about the strange and wonderful creatures that (maybe) lived in faraway lands – now, they were worth reading about.

Stories were told of an animal, with a long nose, that was strong enough to carry a whole castle on its back. (You can probably guess that they must have been talking about an elephant.) Other stories seem to have confused what we know as an antelope, which runs so gracefully and has two horns, with the narwhal, which swims in the Arctic seas and has a single splendid horn. It also features many mythical creatures such as a unicorn, griffin and dragon.

It's lovely (and quite funny) to look at the beautiful old illustrations. But actually what's written is pretty interesting, too. That's because people in the Middle Ages didn't just want to learn about animals; they wanted to learn *from* them. They had this strange (but maybe weirdly very useful) idea that animals are trying to teach us something about ourselves. Cows want us to understand the importance of being patient, they know how to sit quietly in a field, chewing strands of meadow grass and taking each minute as it comes. When squirrels gather nuts in autumn in preparation for the barren winter months when they won't be able to find anything to eat, they are trying to tell us to plan for the future. Lions want to teach us about being more courageous; birds building their nests are trying to send us messages about how home doesn't have to be big to be cosy.

The big idea this kind of book is suggesting is that we can always be learning lessons from nature – remember in the introduction we were talking a little about the writer Beatrix Potter who used a story about mice to teach us that it's OK to be different?

Suppose you were writing a similar book about animals you particularly like. What creatures would you include? And this is the big question – what do those animals represent in your imagination? We've made a start with some animals that mean a lot to us:

ANIMAL	TO ME IT'S SAYING ...
Chihuahua	*that small does not mean cute, it means fierce and loud!*
Dung beetle	*that one creature's waste is another's treasure (or its house, or even its dinner)*
Hedgehog	*that sometimes what's on the outside actually really does count!*

Germany, Around 1455

A Simple but Brilliant Idea about Printing

Remember how earlier, we looked at how people in China were printing multiple copies of books using wooden blocks? It took centuries for this clever idea to be thought of in Europe and, in fact, paper reached Europe before printing (the idea of paper came from China). After the handy invention of paper though, it was only a matter of time before Europeans started trying to think up ways to print so they didn't have to make every book by hand. And it wasn't long before a clever German called Johannes Gutenberg came up with something that changed the world.

 Instead of making big wooden blocks of every single page, why not make a machine with movable, metal letters? The idea behind Gutenberg's printing press was simple, but revolutionary. Here's how it worked: the letters were arranged on a wooden plate (it was very important not to make any spelling mistakes!), covered with ink, then a sheet of paper (or parchment) and a second plate were laid on top. When the two plates were squeezed together, hey presto – a printed page! Gutenberg could print up to 250 pages like this in an hour. And to make a different page, he could just reuse the same letters, rearrange them and repeat the process.

This was a huge step because it meant that it became a lot cheaper (and quicker) to make books. Although a book still cost quite a lot of money – in today's terms maybe as much as a plane ticket or a laptop – that's much, much less than what a book cost before (it cost about the same as a house!). If you had a shop or a farm that was doing quite well you could possibly afford to buy a book. A book was still considered a luxury, but for the first time more people were able to have a book, or even two, at home.

Let's think about what that meant: if more people could own books, or at least get access to them, the number of people who can read (the literacy rate) would start to increase. Then you would get people opening bookshops and more people writing books – because at last you can get a book printed and there's going to be an audience of people to actually read it. Ideas can spread much faster, and you can even send a book from one country to another. You don't need to actually meet someone one-to-one and talk to them; you can write your thoughts in a book and people you've never met can read it and understand what you think – and maybe they'll agree with you. Or perhaps they'll disagree and write *another* book saying why you are wrong. So you start to get more discussion and more debate.

Although Gutenberg is widely credited as the inventor of the printing press, the idea of movable type had actually already been thought of a few centuries earlier in China (although Gutenberg didn't know about it). However, the idea didn't take off in quite the same way for a very good reason: written Chinese has thousands of different characters, compared to the Latin alphabet's mere 26 letters (plus punctuation). Storing and organising individual metal blocks for a Chinese book would have been very complicated, and it would take a long time to set up a page. In western Europe at least, it was as easy as A, B, C …

The Gutenberg Bible, 15th Century

Thinking For Yourself

It's quite hard to imagine, today, how important a single book might have seemed to people in the past. In Europe in the Middle Ages if you were going to read one book in your life, it would almost certainly have been the Christian Bible. Christianity was the dominant religion in most areas of Europe and the Bible contains all the official teachings (rules) and advice for how Christians should live. It is also full of inspiring and helpful stories. However, there was one big problem – very few people could read it. It was written in Latin, the language of Ancient Rome mostly used by scholars (clever people who study a lot), and hardly anyone could read Latin (or any other language for that matter!). Most people relied on priests to read the Bible and tell them what it meant and what to think about it.

Even if more people had been able to read, it would have been hard to get hold of a copy. (Remember the beautiful – and incredibly expensive – illuminated handmade manuscripts from the Middle Ages?) So, now that Gutenberg had developed a movable type, it made sense that one of the first books he would print would be the Bible. Known as 'Gutenberg's Bible', it changed book production forever.

You'll probably never actually read the Gutenberg Bible (even we haven't) but it's worth talking about because it stands for a really important idea. It represents a huge, exciting moment when you start to think for yourself and don't have to always agree with what a grown-up might say.

When you're very little, grown-ups seem to know everything; then gradually you get your own ideas ... maybe the grown-ups can be wrong? Not about everything, just some things.

You're not being naughty or ungrateful: you are following in the great Gutenberg path. Maybe you don't always need your parents or teachers to tell you what to think. Maybe you can take that responsibility for yourself. It doesn't automatically mean your ideas are better – but they are yours. The important thing is that you are starting to think about the complicated questions of what life is all about and work out what you genuinely think.

Thinking can be both exhilarating and challenging at the same time. You're discovering that you can have your own opinion about everything, little and big. You can have ideas about the whole world. But thinking can also be lonely: what if people don't understand, what if people disagree with you, what if some people don't like what you think? And the problem is you grow up in a world where people have lots of ideas (*their ideas*) already. They might be very nice people, maybe they mean well; but still they are talking about how *they* see things and you might see them differently.

With the clever idea of movable type, Gutenberg brought a lot more disagreement into the world (though he didn't mean to). So we need to get smarter about how to deal with disagreement. It's OK to disagree with someone, but it's important to still treat other people's ideas and opinions with respect.

○   What do you and a grown-up not agree on?

○   Why might you be right?

○   Why might they be right?

○   How could you persuade them to agree with you?

○   How might they persuade you to agree with them?

England, 1744

The Invention of Books Just for Children

You've probably had books around you since you were a baby: books that made a 'moo' sound when you pressed a picture of a cow with your tiny fingers or books that you could throw out of your pram for fun, all long before you could recognise or understand any of the words in them. People gave you books as presents, nice grown-ups read you stories and at school they spent ages teaching you how to read. (Do you remember how hard that seemed at first?) And of course, all those books were written and published especially to entertain children and to help them learn. That probably seems obvious; in fact, why are we even mentioning it? Of course there should be books especially for younger readers! But even though it *seems* obvious to *us*, for a very, very long time there were very few books made especially for children.

If parents did read to their children, they read from books written for adults. It may seem unexpected (and perhaps boring) to us now, but in the past a parent might read their child grown-up books about history or religion. They weren't being mean, or even trying to send them to sleep – this is what children read, too, when they were able to read themselves. It was all to do with how people thought about children in general. 'Childhood' itself is a relatively recent concept. Up until around the 18th century, by the time you were about 8 or 9 you were seen as a small adult. If you came from a wealthy family you might be given wine to drink with your lunch and a real sword to carry (if you were a boy); and girls would be expected to wear grand dresses, as if they were going to a ball. And if you were less well off you would be expected to leave school and get a job – maybe working on a farm or helping in a shop.

Things slowly started to change for children around 300 years ago, which is pretty recent considering that humans have been around for hundreds of thousands of years. Grown-ups started to think more about how children might be different from them – and not just in size. They started to realise that maybe it was rather special and interesting to be a child. A child is often more imaginative than an adult – grown-ups sometimes forget how fun it is to play or how to enjoy pretending that the arm of a sofa is a horse. Grown-ups often lose their sense of wonder: they don't marvel at a particularly interesting leaf, or wonder if the Moon feels lonely, or imagine what it would be like if the world was turned upside down and we all lived on the ceiling. Instead of wanting babies to become adults as soon as possible, people started to think that maybe you shouldn't rush to become an adult – you should be allowed quite a long time just to enjoy being a child.

As adults started to take more interest in what might be important to (and for) children, some clever and imaginative adults started to write books especially for younger readers. It's amazing to learn that something that is such a part of our everyday lives today developed so recently, and that for most of history no one thought about writing books for children.

A Little Pretty Pocket-Book Intended for the Instruction and Amusement of Little Master Tommy and Pretty Miss Polly, John Newbery, c. 1744

The Invention of Books Just for Children

This book – thought to be the first book written in English just for children – doesn't sound terribly exciting. But it is the word 'amusement' in the middle of that very long title that makes it so remarkable. 'Instruction' is in there, too, but children would have been used to books trying to teach them things. It's a bit like school – there are things you need to learn, even though they may seem boring or pointless. (We hate to be the ones to say it, but maths is pretty important.) But then there's 'amusement' – having fun, playing, enjoying yourself. Usually teachers don't have to make children do that!

So, this is the first children's book trying to do something huge: it's trying to make instruction (learning) *amusing*. Learning, it's saying, can be enjoyable. You probably know that already – school has changed a lot since the 18th century (although there might be some teachers who need reminding that learning can be fun).

But an even bigger and more amazing idea comes if you think of yourself as the teacher. Actually, you're *already* a teacher in a lot of ways. We don't mean you work in a school of course – that would be weird – but throughout your day you naturally show, explain, instruct and teach others so that they can better understand you and your feelings. That might be explaining what you need, want, and care about to your caregiver, or showing your friends what you like to do. You might, sometimes, have to tell someone that they're upsetting you or you might want to teach a brother or sister to be more tidy. Actually, teaching is one of the most basic and central things we all do because we're always trying to teach other people to understand what we care about.

But, to be honest, sometimes it doesn't go very well. Why? Because we might get frustrated or annoyed and so we tell someone that they are being mean, that they're wrong, that they don't understand anything (and we might stamp our foot and throw in an unkind word or two). We all do it but *of course* it doesn't work. Other people just smile, don't listen or get angry, too and keep on doing their own thing anyway. Remember those two important words in that first children's book? Why are we so bad at *Instruction* – or teaching? The answer is to do with that second big word: *Amusement*. What the first children's book understood was that if you want to teach successfully, it helps if you can make the lesson *enjoyable*.

So, how could that idea help you? Let's think about some situations that you might find yourself in and how you might 'teach' the other person without getting annoyed or frustrated:

I'D LIKE TO TEACH	WHAT I USUALLY DO	WHAT IF I FOLLOWED THE RECIPE: INSTRUCT AND AMUSE?
Dad to listen properly; he just tells me what to do, he doesn't understand what I feel	*Get angry or upset; tell him he doesn't understand anything; slam a door*	*Make a joke: call him 'Captain Magnificent Advice'; give him a cuddle; then say, 'Dad, just listen for a moment.'*
Mum to cook something different	*Whine and say, 'Why can't you cook something nicer?'*	*Say: 'Your banana-and-coffee spaghetti dish is a culinary wonder of the world but I'm worried the other foods (hint: toasted sandwiches) are feeling lonely and left out.' And give Mum a hug, too.*
Over to you …		

Europe, 19th Century

The Industrial Revolution and the Unforeseen Effects of Making Paper

Although the invention of the printing press made books more widely available than ever before, they remained much more expensive than they are today. One of the main reasons for this was the cost of paper. It's so hard to imagine today, but paper used to be a luxury item. So, how could it possibly have been expensive?

To help understand why, you can look at a piece of paper under a microscope. You'll find that it's actually made up of millions of tiny criss-crossing fibres, held together by a special kind of glue. Up until the 19th century, people got these fibres from fabric. They'd boil old clothes in water, shred them, bleach them and then mash them to a pulp. Next, they squeezed out the liquid, added a special glue and spread out the sticky pulp in a very thin layer to dry. After a very long time, it would be a sheet of paper. It was a lot of work to do by hand and it took ages to make a single sheet. And then, on top of this, they started to run out of old clothes to make the paper.

So, where else could they get the right sort of fibres? You're probably already shouting the answer – trees, of course! As we all know now, wood is great for making paper. There's just one tiny problem: it's incredibly hard to mash up a log by hand. Thankfully, the Industrial Revolution, which had begun in the 18th century, was gathering pace in Europe in the 19th century, leading to the invention of all sorts of helpful machines. Soon, it became possible to grind wood into a pulp and make huge rolls of paper much more quickly and cheaply. This brought about huge changes to the world of books. After that you could print, and sell, a book at much lower prices, so many more people could afford to buy them and, therefore, to read them.

Over time it was possible, thanks to these machines, to make paper for a lot of other things, such as wrapping paper, birthday cards, notepads, sticky notes and paper napkins. Eventually billions of trees would be cut down to make all this paper.

Cutting down so many trees is known as deforestation and has had many negative consequences for people around the world and for the environment. However, paper production is not the only cause of deforestation (mining, crop production and cattle farming are a few others) and books undoubtedly have many benefits (that's the whole point of this book). So, the big question is: do you think learning how to make paper from trees was a good thing or a bad thing? And should the people who invented the machines that made it all so much easier be blamed for the unintended consequences of their actions?

Or try it another way: should you be blamed for things you didn't mean to happen even though your actions ended up causing them? Suppose you leave a book on the floor and someone trips over it and hurts their arm? You didn't want them to fall. But they fell because the book was there. And what if it was you who tripped and hurt your arm? What do you think?

These are really tricky questions and not even the cleverest people in the world can be sure of the answers!

Alice's Adventures in Wonderland, Lewis Carroll, 1865

A Friend for When You Feel Confused

One of the consequences of the new, fast and cheap way of making paper was that books started selling in much larger numbers. One of the most successful books was part of the new genre (a fancy word meaning type of book) we mentioned in the last chapter – children's literature. It's a story – not very long – about a young girl called Alice; she's rather curious and has a dream that one sunny, summer afternoon she falls down a very deep rabbit hole and lots of very strange things start happening. She meets a busy white rabbit; she finds herself in a corridor with lots and lots of doors and she doesn't know which one to go through; at one point she grows very tall and then soon after she shrinks to the size of a mouse. She meets all sorts of slightly odd characters, including a cat that disappears until nothing's left but its smile and a rather rude caterpillar. They get angry when there's no good reason or offended when Alice has done nothing except try to be polite. Alice often feels (as she says) 'dreadfully puzzled'.

Of course, it's a totally made-up story. But the story is using made-up things to talk about very real experiences. Feeling puzzled about what's happening in your life or how other people behave, or even about how the world works, is very normal. But we often don't admit just how confused we really feel inside. We think that maybe everybody else understands everything already; we think that it's our fault we feel so puzzled.

This is why it's good to have a literary friend like Alice. She points out things that don't make sense or that she doesn't understand. She shows us that it's not her fault that she's puzzled: lots of things really are confusing and strange, and that it's actually OK (and very clever) to tell people (or white rabbits and large grinning cats) that you can't make sense of them.

And maybe you've got some things of your own that are very sensible to be puzzled about. What might they be? Maybe write them down in a list and then have a chat about them with your friends or family.

○ Why do I have to grow up?

○ Why do our bodies change as we grow up?

○ Why are grown-ups less fun than children?

○ What will I do when I'm older?

○ How do I know if I'm doing the right thing?

○ Is it important to be popular?

A particularly clever thing Alice does is stay calm. She doesn't panic; she's not frightened that she's confused. She's not ashamed to tell people things like 'I don't know what you mean' or 'I don't understand' or 'That doesn't make sense'. Reading her story might encourage you to be more like her.

Feeling puzzled is part of life. Realising and admitting that you don't understand something can be the first step on the path to understanding it!

Europe and the US, 19th Century

What Are Schools For?

Up to about 1800 hardly anyone had any say in how countries were run.

Most people couldn't even vote in elections. In the UK, for example, the right to vote depended on things like whether you owned property or paid certain taxes, even where you lived. It meant that the poorest people were not allowed to vote, so the majority of people did not have any say in who ran their country or what laws were passed. And, as with many things at this time, you had to be a man to take part. (Fortunately, this eventually changed, too.) More and more people started to think, and say out loud, that this system was not fair and should be changed. While some people in the government thought it was the right thing to do, others were worried that if people weren't allowed to vote they'd get angry and start a revolution. (There had been one in France in 1789.) So, it was definitely time for a change.

But there was a big worry. There weren't all that many schools and mostly these new voters would have hardly any formal education at all. Would people understand enough about the world to make good choices? Would they just believe the person who shouted loudest or had the coolest hat?

The answer, most people agreed, was more schools. For a proper democracy (where the government is chosen by the people) in which *all* adults would be allowed to vote, you really need the whole society to be educated. So in the

UK, thousands of new schools were set up and new laws were introduced in the late 1800s saying that, from now on, *all* children would *have to* spend several years in the classroom. No one had ever tried to teach whole nations before. The big question, though, was *what* to teach. Some people said you should mainly teach lessons on art, beauty, wisdom, friendship, kindness, philosophy (our biggest ideas about what life is all about); they thought the goal of education was to make you an interesting, thoughtful and sensitive person.

But there were other people who thought that education in school should be about learning hard facts. There was a big debate in all the most economically developed countries at the time, such as France, the UK, Germany and the US. And all the governments in the end decided that the huge number of new schools would concentrate on getting pupils to answer questions like these:

○ If a circle has a radius of three units, what is its circumference?

○ When did Julius Caesar die?

○ Name the four longest rivers in Africa.

(It's great to know these facts but it's also important to understand other kinds of things as well. How might you have done at a school like that?)

So, the other ideas of education – getting on with people, becoming the most interesting version of yourself, exploring your own ideas, getting wiser, braver or more imaginative – didn't end up in schools but they *were* still in books.

Little Women, Louisa May Alcott, 1868

Learning to Be Wise and True to Yourself

One book that really focused on a more imaginative, alternative kind of education had just been published in the US: it was written by Louisa May Alcott in 1868 and it was called *Little Women*. ('Little' here just means 'young'. Ideas and words change over time and something that could sound a bit unkind to us could actually have been, in the past, a respectful way of speaking.)

A central character in *Little Women* is Josephine, though she prefers Jo. She's 15 when the story starts and has three sisters. A big thing about Jo is that she'd like to do a lot of the things she saw boys do. She likes the sorts of shoes boys wear and how they cut their hair short and she loves dressing up as a pirate. However, in those days girls were expected to wear long dresses and have long hair and be quiet and polite. But Jo wants to climb trees and slap her friends on the back and whistle – which, in those days, were things no 'young lady' was ever supposed to do. Jo feels very different from what was considered to be 'normal'. However, she's pretty good at dealing with the situation. She's lively, funny, loving and (mostly) quite kind. She grows up to be a writer and in fact, she's the narrator (the person telling the story) of *Little Women*: it's her story as told by her.

If wisdom was the main thing taught in schools, there could be a lot of lessons and even an exam based around Jo.

○ How might you become more confident, even if you feel you are a bit different from most people?

○ What would be a good use you could make of your particular talents? (It has to be a use that you believe in and is practically possible.)

○ Jo manages to have a good relationship with her sisters, even though they are so different. Describe how you have managed to have a good relationship with someone who is very different from you.

○ Jo changes her mind about some key things in the story. Describe how you have changed your mind about something important. What led you to change your mind? How do you actually get other people to change their minds?

○ Jo is funny and makes people laugh without being mean. How good are you at doing this? How would you get better at doing it?

Imagine these were the sorts of questions everyone was mainly focusing on in their education, for several hours a day, every day, for years and years. And if you were very good at giving honest answers you'd get top marks and eventually get the best kind of job. And this is what would be admired online. The world would be totally different.

At The School of Life we've got a way of putting this: it's emotional intelligence that the world is short of. That's why as whole societies, we can be anxious, envious and not so good at speaking to people who we see as different. We think that schools should be teaching, and nurturing, wisdom. We hope you might agree and that perhaps one day you'll want to help us try to make the world more wise.

20th Century

Fantasy: A New Kind of Story

By the early 20th century, all the main problems of publishing books had effectively been solved. Printing was easier, paper was cheaper and lots more people – although still not everyone – could read and afford to buy books. Huge numbers of new books were published every year.

So, what were the most popular books? It turned out that many of the most popular books were about *things that aren't real* – they might be books about people who find a cave so deep that it leads to a hidden country or about travelling to the distant future or about elves, wizards and fantastic creatures.

Creating fantasies is one of the strange and wonderful things that our amazing human brains are really good at. It can be great fun to *pretend* to be on a boat surrounded by sharks in the middle of a huge storm, but it would be truly horrendous to actually be in that situation. It's lovely to *imagine* being able to fly just by flapping your arms – but it's really important you don't climb up a ladder and try it out. You have to be really clear about the *difference* between imagining something and what is safe or advisable in the real world.

Generally, it's probably quite easy for you to tell the difference between imagination and reality, but think back to when you were very little. Did you maybe *imagine*, there was a tiger hiding in your cupboard, but then

get frightened and think it was real and not want to open your cupboard? Young children often feel that what they imagine is real. They don't yet understand that their brain has just been busy and that there couldn't really be a tiger in the cupboard. (No matter how many times grown-ups tell them that there is no tiger!)

But it's not only little children. Imagination can be wonderful, but it can sometimes be tricky if you imagine things that aren't very nice. Suppose you get annoyed with a friend and you imagine shouting at them and making them cry. If you *really* did that it would be very bad and you'd be very sorry you did it. But *imagining* doing it is totally different. You don't really *want* to make them cry but your brain just makes up this idea. You haven't actually done anything bad. Imagining making them cry is like imagining a tiger in the cupboard: it's just a picture in your head.

What we're trying to say is that it's normal for not very nice *ideas* to pop into your imagination. And you might feel upset by that. But it's important to remember that there's a really big difference between just imagining something and actually doing it. Just as you might imagine being in charge of the whole world (or living on a cloud) that doesn't at all mean you are planning to actually do these things.

Here are some tricky questions it could be helpful to talk about with a really lovely and very kind grown-up.

○ What are some things you imagine doing or happening?

○ Are there things you worry about because you imagine them?

○ Are there some things you wish you didn't imagine?

The Hobbit, J.R.R.Tolkien, 1937

Smaug, the Dragon

The Hobbit is probably one of the most successful fantasy books of all time; it was written in the 1930s by a Professor of Language and Literature at the University of Oxford called John Ronald Reuel (better known as J. R. R.) Tolkien. It tells of the adventures of a small, hairy-footed, human-like creature called Bilbo Baggins – his main enemy is a huge, scaly, fire-breathing dragon named Smaug who loves stealing other people's treasures and keeping them in his cave.

Smaug the dragon really isn't at all nice: he's greedy and cruel and terribly vain. If people annoy him, he just breathes fire in their direction; if he wants something, he just takes it. Smaug sounds pretty horrible so we know it's going to sound a bit weird if we suggest that maybe you are a bit like him. Of course you don't breathe fire or hoard treasure (do you?) but Smaug represents the mean, I-don't-want-to-share, I-want-all-the-shiny-things part of all of us. Usually it's a small part, but Smaug shows what happens when we allow this part to take over the kinder, nicer, friendlier parts. And maybe Smaug behaves like this because he is frightened and lonely. Maybe what he really needs is a friend.

It might sound a bit far-fetched, but the idea of making friends with Smaug really means making friends with that part of yourself with the unkind or negative feelings. Why might *you* sometimes feel mean and vain? A kind, *friendly* answer is that you feel frightened. You get greedy when you are *frightened* you won't get enough. You get vain (or boastful) when you are *frightened* others won't appreciate you. Breathing fire on people isn't a very helpful response but it might be an understandable response when you feel frightened.

The friendly thing that's going on is this: there's a huge difference between saying someone is not very nice and saying they are frightened. If someone is unkind, you feel they need to be told (quite loudly) to stop being unkind. But if someone is frightened, you think they need to be reassured and helped to feel safe.

Being friendly to the Smaug bit of you doesn't mean saying, 'You're great, go on, keep stealing and keep on terrifying people'. It means saying, 'I know that you are really doing these things because you are lonely and frightened. I'm going to help you by understanding you. You don't really want to be horrible, it's just that at the moment you don't know what else to do'.

○ In what ways might you be (even if just a tiny bit) like Smaug?

○ How do you feel about that part of yourself?

○ What would it be like if you were kinder to your inner Smaug?

Everywhere, Today

Books and Films

Remember we were saying that human beings have always loved stories. Before books came along, people would gather round the fire in the evening and someone who knew the stories very well would pass them on. It must have been an amazing experience, often with the stars overhead, listening to stories of the past, of adventures, of magic. But only a small group of people would hear the story and the story would change a little bit every time it was told.

With the invention of writing and then books, everything changed. Now someone could write down a long and complicated (and very interesting and exciting) story and lots of people could read it. And, with the invention of the printing press, soon thousands of people, sometimes millions, could read the same story. And for a long time books were the most important – and most impressive – way that stories were communicated.

However, over the last 100 years or so (that's actually pretty recent, considering where we started) things have changed because we've also started *watching* stories, as well as reading them (and listening to them). Films started to become hugely popular in the early 20th century. And then really from the 1950s and 60s onwards, television took over. And in the first part of the 21st century online content started to get many, many more viewers than books ever had readers.

The reason *watching* became so big is pretty simple. Reading is something we have to learn – it takes ages and we have to practise and make lots of mistakes before we can do it well. But even babies can watch videos. Our brains just find watching easier than reading.

What this means is that books can't always compete. Of course lots of people still love books, but many *more* people like watching things.

The funny thing is that a lot of *what* people watch actually comes from books. But stories sometimes get changed a bit when they jump from literature to film.

Cinderella (Cendrillon), Charles Perrault, 17th Century

Stories Change over Time

Let's look at how one famous story changed. It's *Cinderella*: the famous story of a kind girl who is treated like a maid and has to sleep in the kitchen. However, she ends up (with the help of a magical fairy godmother) at a royal ball, where she falls in love with a prince and they 'live happily ever after'.

Variations of this story have been told for centuries, but the version you are probably most familiar with comes from the French story *Cendrillon* written in the 17th century by Charles Perrault. He writes about a fairy godmother helping Cinderella and the famous glass slipper that the prince uses to find her. Another famous version of the story is by the German Brothers Grimm, although their version does not have a fairy godmother and is a bit more gruesome! One thing that most versions of the story have in common, including these two, is the presence of Cinderella's stepmother and stepsisters. They treat her very unkindly and don't want her to go to the ball with them.

The story of Cinderella has inspired many plays, operas, pantomimes and films throughout the years. Different details (and songs!) have been added to them but many have had the same idea about the stepsisters. They have made them 'ugly' (whatever that means). Cinderella is beautiful and kind, while her stepsisters are ugly and mean. The message is: beauty = good, ugly = bad. You can probably see the big problems here. Who decides what's beautiful and what isn't? What does the way anyone looks have to do with their personality and behaviour? This can be one of the big differences with visual storytelling, such as films, compared to books. While a written story can tell you loads about someone's feelings or their personality, visual storytelling often has to make this point quickly, in a different way. It can be in the way someone acts, but it can also be shown in the way they look.

Let's think about this idea of the 'ugly' sisters and what it means. Someone who is regularly mean to someone or hurts them with words or actions is a bully. And bullying is never OK. However, it's often the case that bullies are unhappy people acting out their feelings or copying behaviours that they have experienced themselves. Reading this book, you might have some sympathy for the stepsisters – their mum seems pretty mean, so it makes sense that they might copy this behaviour with Cinderella. They don't really know Cinderella and maybe they feel worried or jealous. Good people can end up saying or doing not very nice things when they feel anxious or frightened. Maybe you've felt like this sometimes.

But some films, particularly those aimed at kids, often like to split the world into extremes of totally good and totally nasty people. In Disney's classic animation from 1950, Cinderella is perfect and the stepsisters are awful. There's no chance of sympathising with these stepsisters. (And as for Cinderella, can anyone really be that nice all the time?)

The book versions of Cinderella make space for the idea that you (as the reader) might recognise just a little of the stepsisters in yourself. Some modern Cinderella movies have caught up with this idea, too, giving the stepsisters more personality and showing that they, and their mother, might have some complicated feelings going on. And as for being 'ugly', the only ugly thing about them is their behaviour towards Cinderella.

Saying something unkind that you wish you hadn't, and being consistently unkind are not the same thing. No one is perfect all the time, but someone who is regularly mean to someone or hurts them with words or actions is a bully. The stepsisters bully Cinderella. Do you know anyone like this?

○   Why do you think someone ends up becoming a bully?

○   Do you think a bully might ever wish they could be nice?

PART TWO

LITERATURE AND FEELINGS

Literature and Feelings

If you go into a library, you'll see that the books aren't just placed at random: they are organised. All the books about cooking are together – and so are all the books about history and all the novels. And then these groups of books are arranged alphabetically by author's surname. You can understand why people do this, because often people talk about books in terms of what they are obviously about: this book is about birds, so it belongs in the zoology section next to the other books about birds, or that book is about Roman aqueducts, so it goes in the history section along with all the other books about Ancient Rome.

It's not a terrible idea. But maybe there's a better one. You could say that a book is the answer to a problem. A cookery book could be the answer to the problem, 'I wish I knew how to make an omelette'. A history book could be the answer to the problem, 'I don't know enough about Roman aqueducts'. But a book *could* be an answer to a totally different *kind* of problem: a problem to do with feelings. And it might have nothing at all to do with what a book officially seems to be about.

For instance: an atlas is officially about helping you find out where rivers, capital cities and national borders are. But you could use it to look at the shapes of islands and imagine what your ideal island would be like and who would live there and what they would do. Or if you were feeling upset you might find it calms you down to look at a map of the Kamchatka

Peninsula and imagine the uninhabited forest and swamps and the hills and mountains where the animals live undisturbed. So you might say this is really a book about inspiration or calmness. You are noticing how it helps your feelings and your thoughts.

Imagine sorting your own books out according to how they make you feel. You could place together all the books that make you feel calm, then next to them you could have the books that give you confidence, or books that make you feel excited or curious, then after those you could have the ones that help you when you are feeling lonely or sad.

Or if you think about fiction, it could be that going back to a story you've liked ever since you were little helps when you feel upset.

In this section we're going to be talking about how books can help you understand and talk about your feelings. In each case we'll be suggesting one book that we think is useful, but really there are hundreds. So it's something for you to think about, too: what other books do you think might offer help? For example, what book would you suggest to a friend who is feeling worried or sad, that might bring them a bit of comfort, or to someone who needs encouragement?

Books can be so powerful, helping us through tricky times, offering us wisdom we haven't learnt yet, showing us that there are people like us, or showing us the opposite – that other people live very different lives. Books can be a friend when you need one the most and you can use them to help and inspire others, too.

Reflection

Your brain is very wonderful in lots of ways – but one of its quirks is that it can be forgetful.

And the funny thing is, it's not so much that you forget obscure facts or tiny details – you're more likely to forget really big and obvious things. That sounds strange, doesn't it?

We're not saying you forget the days of the week or the names of the oceans. Rather, what slips the mind are good, important *ideas*. You know that you hate having to do last minute things for school on Sunday evening, but you might end up so often rushing at the last minute to get things done. On Friday and Saturday you *put to the back of your mind* what in a way you actually know. Or, perhaps, you know perfectly well it's not very nice to tease a younger sibling but you keep on doing it because, at the crucial moment, you sort of forget.

In the past people used to write books specifically to remind themselves of things they knew but were always forgetting. The most famous person who did this was a Roman Emperor called Marcus Aurelius who lived in the 2nd century CE. He wrote a little book for himself for his own philosophical guidance and self-improvement called *Meditations*. He tells himself things like: 'Remember to listen carefully to what people tell you, and think about why they might think like that; don't jump in to try to solve a problem until you really know what it is'.

These ideas sound a bit obvious but it's easy to get caught up in things and act without thinking. For Marcus, writing it down helped him to remember to try and do these things. In fact, his book was never intended to be published, but after he died people decided it was so useful that they published it. Nearly 2,000 years later, his advice is still very relevant.

Another thing Marcus likes to remember in *Meditations* is who has been helpful and kind to him. Easy, you might think. But maybe not. The thing is, someone can be nice to you and then also a bit annoying. And it's easy for the annoying things they do and say to sit at the front of your mind. He was reminding himself: someone can be annoying at the moment but, don't forget, you also owe them a lot. It's a bit like the way the person who takes care of you can be irritating and it makes you forget the amazing and important things they do for you every day.

○ If you were writing a little book of instructions to yourself, what might you put in it? (Marcus Aurelius wrote his little book only for himself, and it was only published a long time after his death.)

○ What do you know you should do around friends, your family or in school that you keep sort of forgetting?

The Ten Foot Square Hut, Kamo Chōmei, c. 13th Century

What Makes You Happy, Really?

It can be surprisingly hard to remember what really makes you happy. You keep thinking that if you get more *things* you'll be so happy. Then you do get more things and after a short while you feel just the same as you did before.

Let's meet a very surprising friend, a book by a Japanese writer called Kamo Chōmei who lived around a thousand years ago. Chōmei was a poet who turned his back on society. He lived in a tiny hut, just big enough for a bed, up in the hills, far away from all the fashionable and successful people he knew when he was young.

He wrote a book about how he came to love living in his tiny hut, and how much he enjoyed cooking on his tiny stove and how he liked sitting on his veranda playing music – he had an old Japanese musical instrument that was a bit like a modern guitar. He wasn't very good at playing it but it didn't matter: he didn't have an audience, he was only playing and singing for his own pleasure.

He loved being free. No one was in charge of him. Because he used so few things – he picked berries to eat in the nearby forest, he didn't buy anything, he lit his fire using sticks he'd gathered so he didn't have to pay for energy – he was not always thinking about work and making money.

It can be pretty strange to hear about how happy he was in his tiny home because it goes against all the things we *think* we're supposed to need in order to have a good life.

Although he was writing a very long time ago, Chōmei is still talking to us today. He's reminding us of something we keep on forgetting: we could actually be happy with less.

The book reminds us that being rich doesn't mean having lots of expensive things; it can mean living a calm and happy life with the things you really need. Chōmei is gently reminding you that there can be very nice ways to live that don't have to cost a lot of money. And he's doing that by getting you to focus on what you genuinely enjoy.

○ Imagine your fantasy little hut in which you could live. What would it be like? It might be great to do some drawings.

○ What would you like to spend the day doing?

Happy Crying

Crying when you're happy might sound a bit weird. Most of us cry when we're sad, angry or have hurt ourselves. But there's another kind of crying, too. Have you ever seen a grown-up cry when they're so proud of something you've done or said? Maybe that time you were in your school play, or when your team lost 5–1 but you smiled the whole time, or when you made your mum pancakes on her birthday. They might pretend they have something in their eye or a cold, but really they're crying because they're happy. So, what are these special tears about? They are almost always to do with love, especially the love between family.

Normally, life is a bit complicated: your grown-up might be busy, they might be stressed or upset, they might be tired or away for a while. And you've got lots of things going on in your life that might make you moody or annoyed or just preoccupied. So, love doesn't always get the chance to be properly expressed – lots of little and big things keep getting in the way. But it's there in the background.

Sometimes a book cuts through all these obstacles and describes our underlying feelings. It shows us how much we want and need other people to really care for us and how much we care for them. A book might show us the special moments when people are able to say to each other the very kind and tender things they really feel but so often don't get around to putting into words.

Maybe this is why we cry: because the book is showing us what we really feel. You feel you have to be big and strong and independent, but maybe there's a part of you that just wants to love and be loved.

When a book says the things you wish you could say but never seem to get around to saying, it touches a very deep and special part of who you are.

○ Have you ever seen a grown-up cry like this – about something that seems happy?

○ Why do you think they might be moved to tears?

○ Do you ever feel like that?

○ What might make you feel like that?

○ Would you feel embarrassed if a friend saw you at that moment?

○ Do you think they might (secretly) feel like that sometimes, too?

It's a pity that this wonderful kind of crying isn't talked about more. You might not know if a friend has cried this way, though they surely have. But it is shown to us in some wonderful books, and that's why we love them.

The Little Prince, Antoine de Saint-Exupéry, 1943

A Special Secret about Love

Let's look at a book that has made a lot of people cry in a very interesting way. The book is called *The Little Prince*, and it was written by a French writer called Antoine de Saint-Exupéry, who also flew planes that delivered letters across Europe, Africa and South America.

So, what's it about? It's about a little boy who lives on his own tiny planet. It's so small he can walk right round it in just a few steps. Of course there aren't really any children living on tiny planets (as far as we know). Except that in a way that's what childhood is: you start out only knowing a tiny bit of the world – your house, the area you live in, maybe some of your friends' houses – and to you this feels like it's the whole world.

And on his little planet the boy has just one companion: a rose. He likes watering the rose and seeing it grow and it means so much to him. He loves that rose. A rose? Why a rose? Maybe you aren't that excited by roses. It doesn't matter. The rose here is what's called a 'symbol'. It represents whatever you love very much, someone or something that matters to you.

But then the boy starts to travel, he goes to lots of other planets and one day he finds a place where there are thousands of roses. This is like what happens when you grow older. You discover that the world is huge – and that your little 'planet' of home is only a tiny, minute part of something much, much bigger.

And then there's another shock. Everyone has their own 'rose' and they all think that *their* rose is special and wonderful and may be the best rose ever.

It's a very tricky moment. But then something rather lovely happens in the book. The boy comes to understand that his rose doesn't need to be the best rose; it doesn't need to be the most important flower. What matters is that it's *his* rose. Your loved ones don't have to be brilliant or outstanding in the world to matter to you. What's important is how much care and love they have given you and you have given them.

It's very touching to think that this is a message that has meant so much to so many people that this short book has been translated into more than 500 different languages – more than any other story ever written.

Encouragement

Look at you – you're amazing. You're reading this book and thinking lots of clever thoughts. Maybe you can walk, talk and put your own shoes on and you probably have some really cool skills such as omelette-making, skateboarding, coding or drawing. But you had to *learn* how to do all these things, and we imagine that while you were learning you had lots of encouragement. People telling you to keep trying, that you can do it, saying well done even at your first, less-than-perfect attempts.

Encouragement gives you the confidence to keep trying and practising and it makes you feel good about challenging yourself. Without it, you might feel like you can't do something and might even not want to try at all.

And it's not just physical or practical skills that you might need encouragement with, social or emotional skills can be just as hard and challenging to learn, too. Do you ever feel like you just can't go up to someone and say 'Hello' or put your hand up in class in case you say the wrong thing? Do you not want to dance at a party in case you look silly or wear a cool new top in case other people don't think it looks cool? No matter how many times your grown-ups or friends tell you that you can do it, do you always listen, or do you sometimes feel too shy or embarrassed?

Reading the right book at the right time can be a great source of encouragement, too. Whether that's by reading about someone just like you, by seeing what happens if you listen to the negative voice in your head or being inspired by someone else's achievements.

Of course, there are some things that no amount of encouragement will help you to achieve, such as flying, magic or (probably) scoring the winning goal in the World Cup final, but perhaps there are quite a lot more things you could do, if only you believed you could.

The Boy Who Harnessed the Wind, William Kamkwamba, 2010

You Don't Have to Be a Genius

A great example of an encouraging book is *The Boy Who Harnessed the Wind*. William Kamkwamba, who wrote the book in his teens, grew up in a poor family of farmers in Malawi in south-east Africa. It's about his own, real-life experience.

When William was growing up, Malawi had a big problem: drought. This meant there wasn't enough rain, so the crops couldn't grow and there wasn't enough food for people to eat. Pumping water out of the ground would have helped, but pumps cost lots of money and very few people in Malawi had electricity to power a pump anyway. But William had an idea: it was something he'd read about in a book. He thought they should build a windmill! Most people thought that was a ridiculous idea. Why did William think *he* could solve this problem? He didn't have any money, he didn't have a degree in engineering and he wasn't even a grown-up!

By the way, windmills have been around for hundreds of years and the idea behind them is pretty straightforward. When the wind blows, it moves the blades of the windmill. The blades then turn a shaft inside that can power a machine called a generator, which makes electricity.

Anyway, William didn't give up, even though people thought he wouldn't succeed. He found old bits of metal, broken bicycles and old tractor parts that people had thrown away and then, slowly, worked out how to put them

all together to make a windmill. It looked pretty ramshackle but it did the job. When the wind blew, it generated electricity and then a second machine powered a water pump to help the crops grow.

William had done it! But he wasn't a brilliant inventor or a genius with ideas that no one had ever thought of (and he never claimed to be). Lots of people knew as much – or a lot more – than he did about how windmills work. The difference was that he was brave enough to have a go. He didn't know that it would work, he just thought it *might*.

William is a really encouraging kind of friend to make. He's saying there might actually be solutions to even the most serious problems and you could be the one to find them. The solution doesn't have to be something extraordinary or new, it might actually be quite a simple idea. His true story shows us how to believe in ourselves and our ideas, and to not be afraid to try something new. William's idea changed his and his family's lives. You might not build a windmill, but what might you do that you've been too scared to try?

The Boy Who Harnessed the Wind is just one example of how a book can encourage you. Can you think of any other books you've read that have given you encouragement or might encourage someone else?

A New Perspective

Sometimes, you can't help feeling worried. You might be anxious about a test at school or a problem with your friend, or you might have some big things happening in your life. It can feel overwhelming. But in these moments, you can often find a good friend in a book. Books can help you to feel calmer, less worried or suggest things that you can do to help by giving you a different perspective or viewpoint. They can make you feel understood, that your worries are shared and things will be OK.

One way that books can give you a new perspective is by reminding you about how big the whole world is. When you are able to compare yourself and your life to the vastness of the universe, you may realise (and feel) that what's going on exactly where you happen to be isn't so important.

Have you ever spent time just skimming through a random book, such as one about maps? It might be surprising, but a non-fiction book can be one of the best things to read when you feel upset. Perhaps you pick up an atlas and randomly turn to a page showing the Baltic Sea and focus your attention on the Gulf of Riga. You might notice a tiny island – just a little green blob – called Ruhnu.

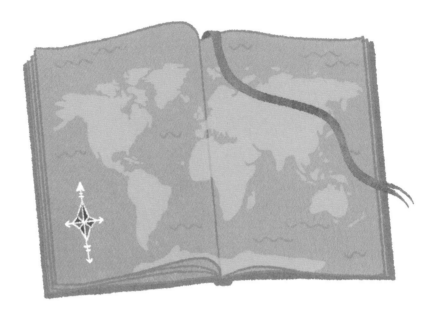

You wonder: what would it be like to live there? Maybe it's practically deserted. Maybe there's a tiny school with only five pupils, and before school you'd get up early in the morning and peer out across the water to see if any ships were around. What would you be eating? What language would you speak? What sort of house would you live in? It doesn't matter if you don't really know anything about it; what's important is that your brain is imagining more and more about a life that's totally different from yours. (The facts are fascinating, too, though: On Ruhnu there used to be a statue of a bear made out of chocolate in the middle of the little village. It looked rather impressive, until the local people ate it).

You could pick any place in the world and imagine what it might be like there. And the funny thing is that when you're doing this, after a few minutes you realise that you've stopped worrying so much. Atlases are just one of the types of books that can remind you how big the world is and how small (in a nice way) you are – which means your worries get smaller, too.

Another way that books can give you perspective is by teaching you about the vastness of time. The world has been around for a very long time and billions of things have happened and will continue to happen. When we are reminded of this, what's worrying you now might not seem like the most important (and worst) thing ever.

Young Dark Emu, Bruce Pascoe, 2018

Two Ways of Looking at the Night Sky

Maybe you don't know much about Australia, the only country that's also a continent. Humans have been living there for around 65,000 years – but not many people outside of Australia knew about the place until some explorers arrived from Europe more than 300 years ago and slowly set about taking it over. They didn't ask the people who already lived in Australia (known as first peoples or Aboriginal Australians) what they thought about this, and with the Europeans' more powerful weapons and soldiers, the first peoples could do very little to stop them.

Soon the whole of Australia, despite being 15,000 kilometres away, became British colonies. The first British settlers were mostly convicts (criminals) transported to Australia because the prisons in Britain were overcrowded. Over time, free settlers arrived, too, and the colonies grew. Eventually, they built roads, farms, towns and cities. They drove the first peoples from their lands, forcing them to find new places to live. The settlers even brought deadly new diseases with them, such as smallpox. The settlers didn't really stop to think about the rights and feelings of the Aboriginal Australians. They were impressed by machines and big buildings – and the Aboriginal people hadn't made any of these things. Did that mean they didn't matter as much? The first settlers thought it meant that they didn't.

This is where Bruce Pascoe's 2019 non-fiction book, *Young Dark Emu*, makes a radical point about different ways of looking at the world.

Normally, when you look at the stars you concentrate on all the tiny, amazing points of light. But what if you got interested in the dark spaces between the stars? This was what the first peoples of Australia did: they saw patterns and meaning in the gaps between the stars and gave them names such as *Gugurmin*, meaning 'Dark Emu'.

In *Young Dark Emu*, Pascoe challenges other perspectives and ideas about Aboriginal Australians and how they lived before the British settlers took over their land. Not everyone agrees with his ideas, but that's OK. The book is so important and interesting because it's giving a new *perspective*. When you read it, you immerse yourself in a way of thinking about the world that's totally different from what you may already know or have been taught. You realise that there are many ways of living, many kinds of things people care about and many different views about the same events or people.

Young Dark Emu is just one perspective. The really important question is what gives you a sense of perspective?

○ What gives you a sense of human experience that's so large that your immediate dilemmas and worries don't feel so big?

○ What stories leave you feeling that maybe it doesn't matter so much what is happening right now?

Guidance

When people want to help you they often give you encouragement. They say you should pursue your dreams and that everything is possible. They are trying to be kind by reminding you that some things might not actually be as difficult as you imagine. That's a good point: we certainly can over-estimate difficulties and that means we give up too quickly on good ideas.

But there's another idea that's important, too: it can also be a problem if you don't realise how difficult something actually is – you try it and find it's much harder than you expected and so you give up.

It's really nice when someone gives you encouragement, but really knowing how difficult something actually is turns out to be pretty important. Imagine you were thinking of climbing a mountain (we're just imagining, we're not at all suggesting you should go off and try this at the weekend).

The thing is, it's really hard to climb a mountain – you need guidance. To do it safely, you need lots of training, to listen to experts and follow their instructions, to save up and buy special equipment, and you need to practise on smaller hills first. You can see they are giving you good guidance: if you know something is hard it doesn't mean you can't do it, it just means you know you need to do a lot of preparation and learn the right skills and eventually you will be able to manage it. Grown-ups are helping you by saying: you know, that is possible but it's also really hard.

It's a funny thing about our human brains: we often need two very different sorts of things at the same time. We need *encouragement* that makes us feel we can do something and *guidance* that explains the genuine difficulties and how (if we pay attention and are patient and make the right effort) we might be able to actually do the thing we want. If you only hear about the difficulties, maybe you'll never bother. But if you only hear people saying 'go for it', you might end up not managing it.

The Analects, Confucius, c.497 BCE

Being Wise about Difficult Tasks

One person who thought a lot about guidance (about explaining what the real difficulties are and how you might deal with them) was someone called Confucius. He lived in China more than two and a half thousand years ago. He came from a once-grand family but they had lost all their money long before he was born so Confucius grew up poor. Later he became a government minister and he had all sorts of interesting plans but the ruling families didn't like his ideas for fair government and education so he became unpopular. For many years, he travelled around looking for people who shared his vision for society.

Confucius was a pretty radical thinker for his time. He believed in wisdom, self-knowledge, courage and social harmony. He acquired some followers and students who shared his ideas but wasn't able to bring about much change in his lifetime. However, after Confucius died his followers collected all his clever sayings to make a book to guide others. It took a few hundred years to get a settled version, but eventually his book, *The Analects*, became very popular and his philosophies were even adopted by China's rulers.

He's got some interesting guidance on how to achieve social harmony (that means everyone living together peacefully). One is that you should spend as much time as you can with people who have more experience. You need to learn from them about what they tried and how it went wrong

and what went well and why. You need to treat them with a lot of respect – otherwise they won't want to pass on what they have learned.

Also, you need to get people to co-operate with you. You can't do any big thing on your own so you need to get other people to understand and (if possible) agree with you. And to do that you have to be very nice to them.

And he also suggested that you should keep your ambitions modest. Why? Because if you learn how to do a small but difficult thing you are developing the skills and the confidence to try something bigger. He thought that good, important changes take a very long time and have to involve many different people. If you want to be the star or want to take all the credit, you will actually get in the way.

What he's saying doesn't sound all that exciting but maybe it's true – and truly helpful. This is just one type of guidance and other books will have other ideas.

○ Have you ever given up on something because it turned out to be much harder than you expected?

○ Is there something other people find difficult that you've learnt to be quite good at? What did you have to do to learn it? (Think as much as you can about this: did you, maybe, have to practise a lot, or listen to feedback from a teacher or coach about all the things you needed to work on, or have to watch other people who were better at it than you or who seemed to find it really easy?

○ Do you think you *could* explain to someone how tricky something really is, without totally putting them off having a go?

○ What would you like guidance on?

Making Hard Subjects Entertaining

It's great to read something that's fun and exciting, where you can't wait to turn the page and find out what happens next. The interesting thing, though, is where entertainment can also be helpful.

A huge problem in the world is that lots of things that are pretty important can often be extremely dull and complicated, so you end up trying to avoid reading about them.

One big example is understanding politics and history. To a lot of people these things can sound quite boring and annoying. Not that many people actually *like* the idea of studying carefully what happened in the past and what's actually happening now around the world and what the proper way of making sense of it all might be. Going into detail and thinking hard is not that entertaining.

Although we *can* use our clever brains when we want to and learn some really tricky stuff (maths, for example), we *much* prefer being entertained. Who doesn't love watching your favourite TV shows or chuckling over cat videos online?

But, as we're sure you've worked out by now, there's a way of being entertained *and* learning stuff you need to. Literature.

Many great works of fiction cover really important and tricky topics by using a really great story to teach or show you something.

Animal Farm, George Orwell, 1945

Making Politics Interesting

Perhaps the funniest and most engaging book ever written about really serious and difficult things is this short novel by an English writer called George Orwell (his real name was Eric Blair, but he used a different name when writing) who lived in the first half of the 20th century. He was a very clever man. When he grew up, he travelled around trying to understand what life was really like for some of the poorest communities. What he experienced inspired him to write several novels. He also wrote about his ideas in newspapers.

Then when he was about 40 he had the clever idea of writing a book inspired by the Russian Revolution of 1917. That might not sound very interesting at all but (and here's the really clever part) Orwell made all the main characters farmyard animals instead of humans. So what seems like an interesting and entertaining story about pigs, dogs, horses and sheep is really about how humans behave.

In *Animal Farm*, Orwell imagines a group of animals having a revolution. They get fed up with their dreary lives just providing food and milk and wool for humans and they chase the farmer away and start trying to run the farm themselves. At first they think it's going to be great but soon it turns out that one group of animals, the pigs, are trying to make things much nicer for themselves at the expense of all the rest.

Through the story Orwell shows how what starts off as everyone being equal soon turns into the pigs being the most powerful. You're reading an entertaining story about animals but – without having to make any big effort – you are also learning a lot about what has actually happened in the world and how some humans behave when they want power. Best of all, this clever book isn't even very long!

You could imagine a test that said: explain how to work out the circumference of a circle *in a funny way*? Or write an *entertaining* essay about the Roman Empire (that's also accurate). It's one of the biggest challenges of life: how to get people to pay attention to important things.

Everyone loves to be entertained. It's pretty crucial that big ideas should come across in an appealing way. Suppose you were inspired by George Orwell. How would you:

○ tell someone you disagreed *in an amusing way*?

○ get someone to enjoy changing their minds?

○ explain that someone was being annoying in a way that made them laugh *and understand*?

Don't worry if there's no immediate answer. These are some of the hardest and most important questions in the world. If you could solve these problems right now, you should probably think about ruling the world (but fairly, of course).

Appreciation for Life

'Appreciation' isn't an everyday word. But it's getting at something important. Because we see it as the opposite of boredom.

Sometimes you might think that the opposite of boredom is entertainment, but that's not the whole story. And you might think that for something to be exciting or entertaining it needs to be extraordinary or something you don't see or do very often, such as bungee jumping or petting a tarantula. However, we think that if you really want to banish boredom, you need to find the joy and entertainment in ordinary things. Really, the opposite of boredom is finding ordinary things interesting. It could be really interesting to just take a look around you and notice the amazing small things. You might watch an army of ants march purposefully across the floor or examine a tree shaped like a wizard. You could sit and watch the world go by outside your window (we've lost *hours* doing this) or just chat about nothing much with your best friends. Maybe these things don't *sound* exciting, but they *can* be very interesting.

'Appreciation' is basically saying that you can see what's fascinating or good about something even though it might seem small or unimportant.

Someone might look at an old person and think they are boring. They wear totally old-fashioned clothes and haven't heard of tons of things and have the silliest phone in the world.

But you might appreciate them. You know that what matters isn't how fancy their phone is or how stylish their haircut isn't – it's their love and kindness. You appreciate how much they care; you appreciate that they *try* and that they are on your side no matter what. You can see what's really lovely about them even if they wear a frock that looks like a sack. They are not boring at all – if you ask the right questions. If you ask them about something you've seen online, they might not have a clue. But if you ask them about what they were like when they were little it could be fascinating.

Appreciation means seeing what might not be obvious to everyone, but once you get to know it you can see that it's lovely. You might appreciate a song that most people don't understand or a painting that no one you know cares about or a book that most people find boring.

○ Can you think of some small things that you appreciate that others might overlook?

○ Can you think of someone else who you can share some of your small joys with?

○ Next time you're walking to school or somewhere you've been a hundred times before, stop for a moment. What do you see?

The Pillow Book, Sei Shōnagon, 11th Century

The Cure for Boredom

Poor Sei Shōnagon – you might think that she lived a terribly boring life. She lived in Japan more than a thousand years ago, at the court of the emperor, which might sound fancy. However, it meant (in those days) that her life was regulated all the time: she could hardly go out of her room, she certainly couldn't leave the palace and she had to be always waiting around in case the emperor or the empress wanted her for something – to play a word game or tell jokey bits of gossip – which wasn't that often. The highlight of her year was going on a short trip to hear a lecture.

It sounds boring but the strange fact is that she wasn't bored at all. Maybe not much was going on but she took a lot of interest in the little things that did happen. We know because she wrote a fascinating book about her life, which became known as *The Pillow Book*. Nobody really knows why it's called that, but we like to think it's because she kept it under her pillow and would sometimes add to it in the middle of the night.

In the book, she doesn't describe what happened that day, instead she asks herself questions – she'll say to herself something like, 'What weather do you like best?' And then try to answer her own question by saying something like: 'It's complicated because actually there are nice things about all sorts of different weather. It can be lovely seeing the frost on a tree or hearing the rain on the roof'. Or she'll ask herself: 'What's nice about someone's trousers? What's amazing about how someone walks? What's funny

What makes me FEEL embarrassed?
What are the BEST smells?
What are FIVE of my FAVOURITE Words?
What Weather do I like Best?

about what someone said? What's your favourite name for a river? When you hear the word "autumn" what do you think of? Why are some trees nicer than others? What makes me feel embarrassed? What do you see other people doing that you'd like to do?' (Sei Shōnagon herself was intrigued by what it would be like to conduct a band or manoeuvre a huge crate through a narrow gate.)

It might not seem like much, but really it's a huge thing. Asking yourself questions and really trying to answer them is the antidote to boredom. In the inspiring spirit of Sei Shōnagon you could ask yourself some questions:

○ What are five of your favourite words? And what is it about them that you like? (To give you a bit of encouragement we asked ourselves the same question: the top words were 'little', 'sweet', 'simple', 'ambivalent' and 'because'.

○ What are the nicest trousers? And who wears them? How do they feel about wearing them?

○ Who is the funniest person you know? What funny things have they said or done? Why did you find those things so entertaining?

Growing Up

Every day we all get a little bit older (and wiser, hopefully). And maybe part of you is desperate to be older so you can do whatever you like, but maybe another part of you misses the simple fun of being 5 years old. School was just about playing and people thought you were amazing just for counting to ten. As you get older, life gets a bit more complicated and, sometimes, a bit less fun.

But growing up doesn't mean letting go of all the fun of being a kid. Have you ever found something that you used to really like when you were younger: a toy you loved playing with or a book that was special? You get a happy feeling when you remember the fun you had with it. Hold on to those feelings, all the fun and memories of being little are still inside, nesting like one of those Russian dolls. And maybe, even though you're cool and wise now, let that little kid out sometimes to just have fun.
Even grown-ups know how to have fun, sometimes.

As you grow older you don't have to leave your childhood behind forever. That wonder and joy will still be there deep inside you.

Peter Pan and Wendy, J. M. Barrie, 1911

What's Good (or Not so Good) about Being Young?

Peter Pan is a magical boy: he can fly, he wears clothes made of leaves and he's brilliant at sword-fighting. But the main thing about Peter is that he never grows up: he's always, forever going to be a child; he'll never have to become a teenager or an adult.

It's a lovely book with lots of exciting adventures – maybe the nicest bit is when Peter teaches some children how to fly, which would be amazing if it could really happen.

But really the book is asking you a huge question: are you worried about having to grow up? You don't think about this at all when you are 3. As you get older you start to realise: one day you are going to be big. Is that exciting or is it scary – or a bit of both? Would it be perfect to be like Peter and always stay a child or is it great to get older? What do you think? How do you feel about it? What's it going to be like to be 15 or 25 or 47 or 74?

Peter Pan and Wendy isn't really saying you (like Peter) won't grow up: that's impossible. But it's saying something more useful: that even though you *do* (of course) grow up, you don't have to lose touch with your childhood self. Growing up doesn't have to mean forgetting what it's like to be (and what's nice about being) little. The solution isn't staying a child forever but becoming an adult who likes the childlike parts of themselves.

○   What's nice about being a child?

○   What's a bit of a problem with being a child?

○   What could be great about being a grown-up?

○   What might be tricky about being a grown-up?

And you might like to talk about your answers with a favourite grown-up. They might have some ideas of their own to share!

Friendship

Life usually feels a bit easier when you have a friend by your side. Someone (or a whole group of them) to navigate school with, to chat with, play with and talk about your favourite things with. Someone who just gets you (and you get them).

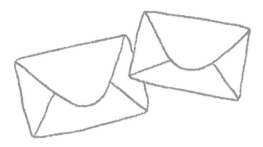

A friend isn't just someone you can do fun things with either – although that's great, of course. Friends support each other when things don't go so well, too. Friends help each other when they are sad or upset, or having a difficult time. They listen and understand, and they can always be trusted with your deepest secrets.

Without friends, life can feel a bit lonely. But, it can also feel lonely if you don't have the right kind of friends either, the good ones who really care about you. They might be quite nice in some ways but you feel that if you tried to tell them about what's really going on in your life they wouldn't really know what you were talking about, or that there are important parts of you that they can't understand. You feel they wouldn't be properly sympathetic, they wouldn't genuinely be interested. So you shut down parts of who you are when you are around them.

But sometimes you might need a different kind of friend, or sometimes you might have no friends around when you need them. And, as we've said before, you can always find a friend in a book. One famous writer found a very clever way to make friends when she was in a difficult situation – she made her own book.

The Diary of a Young Girl, Anne Frank, 1947

How Imaginary Friends Can Help You

This is a true story about a girl called Anne who lived in Amsterdam, the Netherlands, in the 1930s and 40s. For her 13th birthday (12th June 1942) she was given a lovely little book with a red-and-white checked cover but all the pages were blank: it wasn't for her to read but to write in. So she started writing a diary.

While Anne was writing her diary the Second World War was going on and the German Army invaded the Netherlands. Her family were Jewish and the Nazi government in Germany had lots of unfair and horrible rules about what Jewish people could and couldn't do. It was very scary and dangerous to be Jewish at this time. So, Anne's family and some of their friends went into hiding in some secret rooms above the warehouse of her father's business.

Anne stayed there for two years. It was a very strange time: never being able to go out, never being able to even look out of the window (in case someone saw her), always with the same few people. And all that time she kept writing to 'Kitty' in her diary.

Anne was quite clever, lively and rather talkative – the teachers in her class were always having to ask her to be quiet. And she was popular, too: other children were always interested in riding their bikes home with her after school. But, all the same, Anne was lonely.

In her diary she has a very interesting idea: she *invents a friend* who she decides to call Kitty. In her diary she tells Kitty about all the things that she's secretly feeling and thinking – and she never shows her diary to anyone. 'Kitty' is the only person with whom she can be really honest.

Anne can tell Kitty what she feels about her mother and her mother's friends; she talks about a boy called Peter who at first she thinks is rather boring but then starts to get interested in; she talks about the other girls at school and who she likes and who she thinks is silly or a show-off. And, as Anne imagines it, Kitty always understands perfectly and sympathises, and is always interested in hearing more.

Some people might think that having an imaginary friend is babyish and a bit silly. But Anne needed a friend to help her through a terrible situation. This made-up person, Kitty, is doing a very important job: she's helping Anne explore her very real, and sometimes tricky, thoughts and feelings.

○   If you were making up an imaginary friend to be totally honest with, what might they be like?

○   What would you call them?

○   What would you want to explain to them?

You could even try – very privately – writing a diary or some letters to this person telling them about your life and what's really going on in your mind, because you know they will understand.

If you think about it, Kitty and Anne aren't two different people. They are actually showing you the two different sides of being a friend. One is the Anne part where you get brave enough to tell another person about your feelings or secrets. The other is the Kitty part that's kind enough and interested enough to really listen properly. In a good friendship you actually do both things: you are like Anne when you tell your friend about the things that matter to you; and you are *also* like Kitty when you listen very carefully – and sympathetically – to what your friend tells you about what matters to them. And that's the big, wonderful secret of true friendship.

And you might be wondering what happened to Anne. Unfortunately, she did not live to see her important book published or to see how much it helped and inspired others. When the Second World War was nearly over (and Anne would have been able to come out of hiding), the most terrible thing happened. The German soldiers found where she and her family were hiding. Only her father survived. When he came back to the hidden rooms he found Anne's diary. He must have been sadder than anyone can imagine. But he knew that what Anne had written was very beautiful and important and later the diary was published and became very famous.

But one of the things literature does is that it keeps good things alive – Anne's words, and her lovely invented friend Kitty, who she needed so much, have survived. And they always will – wherever there is loneliness and the longing for true friendship.

WHY DO YOU LIKE YOUR FAVOURITE BOOKS?

Why Do You Like Your Favourite Books?

Before we think about why you like your favourite books, let's start by finding out which books they are. Think of a few books you like (you don't need to decide which is your absolute favourite) and write them down in the first column.

Then, write what you like about these books – write as much or as little as you like.

A BOOK I LIKE	I LIKE IT BECAUSE ...

Did you find that second bit much harder? Lots of people do! When you ask yourself why you like a book, your mind might go a bit blank at first. You know you like it, and you know there must be very good reasons why you like it – but just now you can't think *exactly* what they are. Your brain doesn't always tell you *why* it likes things. You might say 'It's great', 'It's exciting' or 'It's lovely'. These are all ways of saying *how much* you like it, but they don't describe what it is that fascinates or delights or pleases or moves you.

Just keep on pushing your brain gently:

○ If you say the story is exciting, try to say *what* is exciting about it. What happened in the story that made you feel excited?

○ If you really liked one of the characters, try to say *what* you like about them. Are they brave or funny or kind or do they say very interesting things? Go into as much detail as you can.

○ Think about what the story might be trying to teach you. Why is this a nice lesson for you to learn or be reminded of?

Sometimes it's much easier to think about why we don't like something than to explain why we do. But thinking about why we like something is very useful. It can help you to understand important and interesting things about yourself.

And here's a secret: people who *write* books have probably spent a lot of time thinking about what they love about *their* favourite books. And when they write, they carry all those wonderful books with them and try to make a book that *you* will love as much.

THE FUTURE OF BOOKS

The Future of Books

Way back at the beginning of this book, we talked about the first books. Over the centuries, books have developed from clay tablets to papyrus scrolls, handwritten parchments to the paper books we see today. Books have changed a lot over time already, but you can still see many of the ancient books in museums (although they probably won't let you read them). Today, many people read books on electronic tablets (so, the Mesopotamians were right about tablets) and maybe one day paper books will even disappear.

But it's not just the physical appearance of books that has changed over time – the subjects have changed, too. Most medieval books in Europe were about Christianity, while books written especially for children weren't introduced until the 18th century. The first book with photographs in it was published in 1843 (it was about algae). Nowadays you can probably find a book about any subject you can think of.

So, what sorts of books might there be in the future? Of course, we don't *know* – but here are some ideas about the kinds of books we'd like to see.

1. A Book That Knows When You Need It

Quite often you might read something very helpful, when you are tucked up in bed at night: maybe in your bedtime story someone gets cross with their mum but then remembers all the things she does to help them and that reminds them why they love her so much. The next day you get cross with *your* mum. If only you were reading that bit of the book at that moment! But the book is sitting on the bedside table and you're not thinking about

it just now. Maybe in the future that book could send a message to your brain saying, 'Remember what I was saying last night!' The technology might be a bit tricky today (how could the book know you were cross with your mum? How would it beam a message into your brain?), but who's to say that *you* won't go on to invent it!

It could ideally be a bit like satnav in the car. The satnav knows where the car is and can give the driver good instructions at just the right moment: turn left at the roundabout, now keep going straight for 400 metres. But this would be satnav for your life. The book would know where you were in terms of your thoughts and feelings, and could give you useful advice just when you needed it.

2. A Book That Can Answer Your Questions

Have you ever come across a footnote? Here's one.[1] Most books don't have them, but sometimes when you are reading there might be something that you don't quite understand and you wish you could just ask the writer: 'Why did you say that? What do you mean? Can you explain it another way?'[2] You can't have footnotes for everything, though. In terms of paper printing, it would be terribly wasteful. In the future, rather than having a footnote, perhaps you will be able to ask the book and it will speak back to you. A book could have hundreds of footnotes that it would only tell you about if you happened to ask.

---

1   Hello, I'm a footnote. You might find me at the bottom of the page or sometimes at the back of the book.
2   Footnotes often include background information or tell you about other related books.

Sometimes, you might feel that a book doesn't tell you enough. *The Boy at the Back of the Class* by Onjali Raúf (see p.14) is about a mysterious new student who sits quietly at the back of the class, but no one knows why (at first). In the story, there's a bully who is really horrible to the new boy (and lots of other people). But we never find out *why* this bully is so mean. However, with our wonderful new (imaginary) technology you could just ask: 'What happened to this person to make them so unkind? They couldn't have been born mean. Babies aren't bullies. So, how did they become this way?' It would be really helpful to understand (although not really relevant to the main story). So, until the new technology arrives you just have to have a go yourself. In fact that's a lot of what you do when you read something very carefully – you think about all the things the writer doesn't get round to telling you.

3. A Book That Is Written Just for You

In an ideal world you would read the perfect book that had been written just for you. The person who wrote it would know you very well; they would know exactly what you like, but also what ideas could really interest and help you. Maybe it would be a story in which you were the central character.

It's a lovely idea and in the past, a few books like that were actually written. An interesting example of this is *The Adventures of Telemachus*, published in 1699 by one of the greatest French writers, François Fénelon. He wrote it for his pupil, who was only 7 years old at the time. The circumstances surrounding the writing of this book were extremely unusual. Fénelon's pupil was the grandson of Louis XIV, the king of France, and the richest and most powerful sovereign of that era. Everyone expected that one day the little boy would become king, too, so Fénelon wrote a story in which he and the young prince travelled around the world visiting lots of different countries and seeing how they were governed. The idea was to teach his young pupil, in a very charming way, about how to be a good king.

In many ways it's a brilliant and useful idea – but you can understand why there aren't many books written specifically for just one reader. You wouldn't sell many copies!

Maybe technology can change this. Making a book personal is a kind of translation. Computers can already translate one language into another. Perhaps, instead of being translated into Spanish or Korean, a book could be translated into the language of *you*. You could take any book and use the 'translate to me' function and it would appear on your screen adapted precisely for you. The central character would be facing the same issues you do and the people around them would be like the people around you. It would present you with the writer's best ideas about how to help you. Whether you would find them useful, or even interesting, might be another matter though!

4. A Book That Can Mix Up Other Stories

Sometimes there's a character in one book that you really like, and you wish you could meet them in other situations. Suppose you've been reading Roald Dahl's *Charlie and the Chocolate Factory* and you quite like Charlie as a character – but by now you've heard enough about the chocolate factory and you wonder what it would be like if Charlie were in your class or if he was your next-door neighbour and had a pet dog. You could imagine an amazing future technology that could take a character out of one story and insert them into another one.

Or what if this wonderful technology could put *you* into a story. It could add you into *Alice's Adventures in Wonderland* (though the title would have to change; it would have to become Alice's and [your name]'s Adventures in Wonderland. And the story would change, too, because you'd do and say all sorts of clever things that aren't in the original book.

We don't really have a computer program that can do this yet. But there is already one very special, super powerful machine that can manage it: your brain and your imagination. You could write a story that mixes up characters from loads of your favourite books!

5. A Book That's Written by You and Published for Friends and Family

Maybe you don't think you are a writer – but you are already, even if you don't know it. Because you often do the same sorts of things writers do. You might imagine what it would be like if you were in very different situations: what if you were stuck in a research base in Antarctica during a storm? What if you were the size of a mouse and could explore in all sorts of tiny spaces? What if you lived in a treehouse?

Or you might think about what it's like to be someone else. What might it be like to be a politician, or a teacher or a scientist? What would you do; what might happen? What would you worry about? What would be interesting?

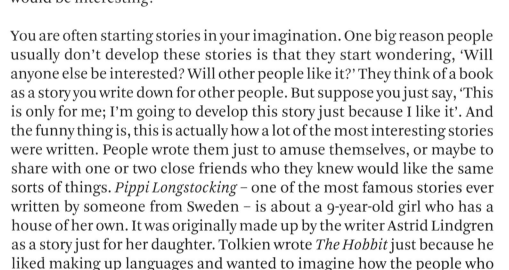

You are often starting stories in your imagination. One big reason people usually don't develop these stories is that they start wondering, 'Will anyone else be interested? Will other people like it?' They think of a book as a story you write down for other people. But suppose you just say, 'This is only for me; I'm going to develop this story just because I like it'. And the funny thing is, this is actually how a lot of the most interesting stories were written. People wrote them just to amuse themselves, or maybe to share with one or two close friends who they knew would like the same sorts of things. *Pippi Longstocking* – one of the most famous stories ever written by someone from Sweden – is about a 9-year-old girl who has a house of her own. It was originally made up by the writer Astrid Lindgren as a story just for her daughter. Tolkien wrote *The Hobbit* just because he liked making up languages and wanted to imagine how the people who spoke those languages would live and what they would do. He also liked telling a few friends about his made-up world. These writers must have been very surprised when it turned out that lots of other people happened to like their stories, too. They often wrote to entertain their own children, and you could start by writing to entertain your friends or family, too.

We tend to think that the way things are now is the way they are always going to be and that all the interesting things have already happened. But it's more reasonable to think that we're still in the early stages when it comes to literature. Human beings have been around for hundreds of thousands of years, but the first books were only made a few thousand years ago and books only became a normal part of life in the last couple of hundred years. Two hundred years is practically nothing in the long story of existence – books and stories have hardly got started! In another hundred or so years, people might look back at us and think that we were still in the Stone Age, as far as literature is concerned.

We're excited about the future of books, and we hope that you'll want to be one of the people who helps to write and create – and read – the books we all need. Please join in!

MAKING FRIENDS WITH BOOKS

Making Friends with Books

There are lots and lots of books and stories in the world – and sometimes people think that you need to read as many of them as possible. They go around saying, 'Have you read this?' or 'Have you read that?' They think what matters is *how much* you have read.

But there's another idea that we prefer. Books are like friends. A good friend understands you and shows you all sorts of interesting things; you like being around them. But you don't necessarily need a lot of friends – even finding one genuinely good friend is great. And maybe it's the same with books: it's better to find a few books that really mean a lot to you and spend a lot of time with them. You might want to read them again and again just because you enjoy being in their company.

We've been introducing you to some of the literature we're friends with and we hope that, along the way, you have met one or two stories that you might like to make friends with, too. Books are friends who will stick with you and help you and encourage you (and sometimes make you laugh) today and into the future.

MY FAVOURITE BOOKS

TITLE	AUTHOR

What are YOUR Big Ideas?

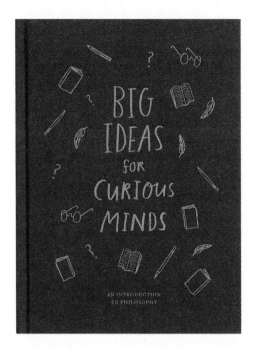

Big Ideas for Curious Minds

An introduction to philosophy

Children are, in many ways, born philosophers. Without prompting, they ask some of the largest questions: about time, mortality, happiness and the meaning of it all. Yet sadly, too often, this inborn curiosity is not developed and, with age, the questions fall away.

Big Ideas for Curious Minds is designed to harness children's spontaneous philosophical instinct and to develop it through introductions to some of the most vibrant and essential philosophical ideas of history. The book takes us to meet leading figures of philosophy from around the world and from all eras—and shows us how their ideas continue to matter.

ISBN: 978-1-9997471-4-5

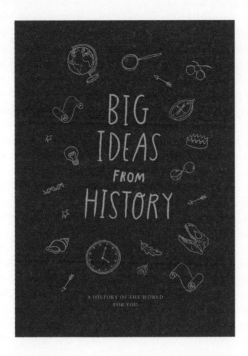

Big Ideas from History

A history of the world for you

The present can loom very large in a child's mind: all the challenges of the modern world can feel overwhelming and, at times, dispiriting. *Big Ideas from History* is an immense story of what has happened through time, from the beginnings of the universe to now, that speaks personally and constructively to a growing mind.

The book encourages children to think about how and why they experience the world as they do and offers a helpful perspective by placing their thoughts and feelings in the context of our history. What might the dinosaurs or the Ancient Egyptians, the Aztec warriors or the Enlightenment thinkers of the 18th century tell us that could be interesting and useful to hear now? The book also looks to the future and asks the reader to imagine a world they would like to live in. It is a thoughtful and inspiring introduction to the world around us, which encourages the child to engage with themselves and others through history.

ISBN: 978-1-912891-80-19

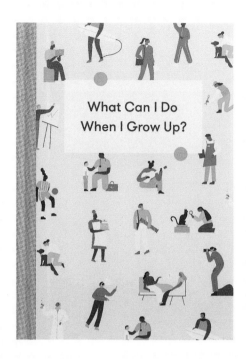

What Can I Do When I Grow Up?

A young person's guide to careers, money – and the future

Have you ever felt confused, scared or even a little annoyed when an adult has asked, as if it were the most normal thing in the world: What do you want to do when you grow up? If so, you are not alone. Knowing what you want to do with your life is one of the hardest questions you will ever have to answer and it's one that most adults are still grappling with...

What Can I Do When I Grow Up is a book about the world of work written expressly for young people. It takes us on a journey around the most essential questions within the topic, such as: *How can I discover my passions? What should a 'good' job involve? How much money should I make? How does the economy work?*

The result is a book that will spark exceptionally fruitful conversations and help you look forward to your work life with positivity and anticipation.

ISBN: 978-1-912891-20-7

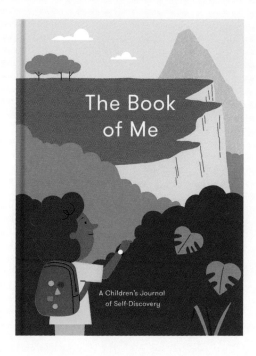

The Book of Me

A children's journal of self-discovery

Children love to explore, born with a boundless desire to understand the world around them. While most of the outside world has already been mapped, there's a whole other world that has yet to be discovered, one that's accessible only to them: their own minds.

The Book of Me is a guided journal of self-discovery. It takes readers on a journey inside themselves, helping them explore their mind, their moods, their imagination, their conscience, and how they determine the course of their lives. Alongside wise and engaging explanations of ideas, each chapter contains a wealth of interactive exercises that together help to create a rich and unique self-portrait. Through writing, drawing, cutting out and colouring in, children can begin to untangle the mysteries of existence and work out who they really are (and who they might become...).

ISBN: 978-1-912891-61-0

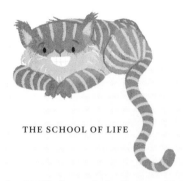

THE SCHOOL OF LIFE

The School of Life is a global organisation helping people lead more fulfilled lives. It is a resource for helping us understand ourselves, for improving our relationships, our careers and our social lives – as well as for helping us find calm and get more out of our leisure hours.

We do this through films, workshops, books and gifts – and provide a warm and supportive community. You can find us online, in stores and in welcoming spaces around the globe.

www.theschooloflife.com